Doodle
ZEN

KEEP

calm

~ AND ~

DOODLE
ON!

Doodle

ZEN

FINDING CREATIVITY
AND CALM IN A
SKETCHBOOK

Dawn DeVries Sokol

STC Craft | New York

Published in 2016 by Stewart, Tabori & Chang
An imprint of ABRAMS

Library of Congress Control Number: 2015948557
ISBN: 978-1-61769-191-1

Editor: Cristina Garces
Designer: Dawn DeVries Sokol
Production Manager: Katie Gaffney

The text of this book was composed in Litterbox and Courier New.

Printed and bound in the United States

10 9 8 7 6 5 4 3 2 1

Stewart, Tabori & Chang books are available at special discounts when purchased in quantity for premiums and promotions as well as fundraising or educational use. Special editions can also be created to specification. For details, contact specialsales@abramsbooks.com or the address below.

ABRAMS
THE ART OF BOOKS SINCE 1949
115 West 18th Street
New York, NY 10011
www.abramsbooks.com

if Found,
PLEASE RETURN TO:

Contents

INTRODUCTION

"Slow down."

How often do you hear these words or think them to yourself? You're not alone. In this high-tech, fast-paced world, we often find ourselves a bit out of sorts, struggling to keep up.

Years ago, I started to experience panic attacks—full-blown, mind-numbing bouts of a drowning sensation—brought on by the sudden death of my father. By this time, I had already begun my artistic journey by exploring my more creative side in art workshops and mixed-media classes, but this was the catalyst for me to begin using art as a respite when life became overwhelming.

I don't want to say doodling alone saved me (I also sought my doctor's advice, which helped quell the panic attacks) but it did give me an outlet to express myself and find calm when I felt I couldn't otherwise. In life, anxiety is something that will always come and go, and you learn ways to deal with it. For me, doodling is part of that process: I go to my sketchbook, and I create. I put on some music and take a line for a walk. Doodling calms me and soothes my soul, as corny as that may sound. Zoning out for just a little while on something creative can make a big difference during difficult times.

Doodling is a relaxing, meditative activity that steers me onto the imaginative highway in my brain. Venturing to this other place often helps when I've hit a creative rut. Doodling breaks me free from thinking too much and letting negativity take over.

This is my sixth doodling book, and by now I'd call myself a huge proponent of doodling. I wanted this tome to focus on the calming side of doodling and to show you some ways to relax through your pen. For me, doodling is just that: making random marks on a surface with a pen, or even a brush. It's not copying others' work, following a "pattern," or employing a prescriptive set of circles and lines to create a design. Doodling is a free-flow process, using scribbles and various marks to decompress. Not only do I doodle shapes and marks, but I also include words in journal-like ways, and even some collage as well. All is fair game in my sketchbook. After DOODLE ZEN, it will be in yours, too. Every prompt in this book is designed to loosen you up and get you into a creative groove. Don't worry about the outcome of your marks. Expectations can hinder the process. In other words, your marks and doodles don't have to look "perfect." We will talk about repetition to refine doodles, but we will also create scribbly, childlike doodles as well. We'll make a mess. We'll PLAY!

Above all, we'll kick back, have fun, and discover our creative zen.

HOW tO USE tHiS BOOK

- Take a deep breath before you do ANYTHING. Remember, it's just doodling! It's just you and a pen playing around.

- Trust yourself and your hand. There is no right or wrong way to discover calm with this sketchbook.

- Do not overanalyze the prompts. Go with your gut, and just let your pen move across the pages.

- If you know of others creating in their own copies of this book, don't compare. Too often, we think that someone else's way of drawing or doodling is better than ours, or it's the "right" way. There is no right way. Just your way.

- I offer a list of supplies, but there isn't any requirement for what you use. You can find your way with just a pencil or ballpoint pen if you'd like.

- You might wish to do one of the prompts again or doodle something of your own. Some pages contain only colored backgrounds or short quotes so you can do just that.

- When you need that extra push, I have sprinkled a few pages with "doodle starters" throughout the book. These are little doodles for you to add on to, just to get you going.

- Skip around in this book if you want. You don't have to doodle through it from beginning to end. Personally, I never create in my sketchbooks in any sort of order—I bounce all over the place, going from one page in the back, to one in the front, to one in the middle. I stop at whatever page feels good at the time and doodle there.

- Never take anything too literally. If you start to wander in a different direction than the given prompt, no sweat! It's YOUR book. Do what YOU want with it!

Supplies

THE DOODLE TOOLBOX

You don't need to buy a ton of supplies to enjoy this book; tools are secondary to the creating. Your tool can be just a ballpoint pen or pencil. But, if new materials inspire you, here are my recommendations for adding some variety to your doodling toolbox:

Black felt-tip pens

Sakura Pigma Micron pens are my preference for basic black doodling. There are many different sizes of tips; my favorites are .03, .05, and .08. For thinner lines, try .01 or .03. For thicker lines, try .05 or .08. The brush tips are great for filling in large areas or for doodling extremely thick lines.

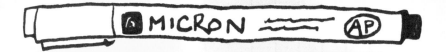

Gel pens

I like to use Sakura Soufflé and Glaze pens for adding in color and/or filling in areas of my doodles. The Glaze pens are translucent and jewel-like, while the pastel Soufflés dry on the paper as a raised, yummy opaque layer.

White pens

White pens are perfect for doodling over darker background colors. However, not all white pens are made to write over painted surfaces. The Signo UM-153 is a Japanese pen with white ink that flows well over pages that have already been painted on. I buy mine on JetPens.com, but these once hard-to-find pens are now becoming more available at US scrapbooking and craft stores. White correction fluid pens or white Sakura Soufflé gel pens also work well, but they won't offer the same solid, fluid line as the Signo.

13

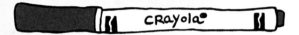

Markers

Tombow Dual Brush Pens contain a different tip at each end and come in a wide variety of luscious colors. Crayola Washable Markers are an inexpensive alternative, are widely available in big-box stores, and have color quality comparable to the Tombows.

pencils

An old No. 2 will suffice in a pinch, but there are also some other great alternatives that I often fall back on. Graphite drawing pencils come in a variety of shades and can be used to create a host of different effects. The mid-range HB is my go-to pencil. Stabilo All pencils create an intense black line on your pages, and can be smudged with a bit of water to develop mono effects.

OIL PASTEL

Crayons

Regular crayons, such as Crayola, lend a textured look to your doodles. You can also use Crayola Oil Pastels with a lighter hand, but make sure to smear them into the page, otherwise they may rub off onto the facing page. Other alternatives include Caran d'Ache Neocolor II pastels (a bit more expensive, but long lasting) available at art-supply stores à la carte, which is a great way to try out your favorite colors. The NeoColors are firmer than oil pastels, but you can still smudge them into the page. Both are water-soluble.

colored pencils/ watercolor pencils

I stick with Derwent Inktense pencils, which work equally well as colored or watercolor pencils. Leave them dry or smudge them with just a tiny bit of water and the color jumps off the page.

ENGLAND DERWENT·INKTENSE

Adhesives

My go-to adhesive is Tombow MONO Permanent Adhesive because it's easy to take along with you. The glue is applied to the surface through a tape roller, so there's no mess, and the adhesive holds well for dry layering. Any glue stick will work as well, but I prefer the Tombow MONO. Neither one will seep out from underneath collage bits like regular glue, so pages won't stick together later.

Instead of adhesives, you can also use paper clips, stickers, photo corners, brads, staples, pretty paper tapes (called Washi tapes), or even Scotch tape. All are great alternatives and add a different look to your pages.

GLUE STICK

Ephemera

Your journal should be a reflection of your everyday life, and collecting and pasting in bits and pieces from your travels is a great

way to add dimension and make these pages your own. Hold on to candy wrappers, receipts, labels, fruit stickers—anything that moves you. For an even more personal touch, make photocopies of old family photos to use in collages, even if they are black and white, since color copies retain the quality and tint of the original.

Scissors

Even though we are primarily doodling, we'll also be exploring a little collage, so you might want to acquire a good pair of scissors. I love scissors that are small, so they're easy to transport, and the smaller tips allow you to make very fine cuts and get into hard-to-reach places. They also have a nonstick surface, so you can cut sticky items without worrying about adhesive residue. Try the Fiskars Nonstick Titanium Softgrip Detail Scissors or Fiskars Crafts Teresa Collins Non-Stick Fashion Scissors.

What art offers
is SPACE — A CERTAIN
breathing room
FOR THE SPIRIT.
~ John Updike

18

chapter 1

Exercising the Muscle

In this section, we'll doodle with basic shapes, allow paint spots to influence our doodles, and work our way into some more complex, continuous doodling from page to page. These prompts will allow you to look inward and learn to loosen up your hands. Just breathe and go with the flow.

IN THE Round

Doodle only circles.

IDEA SPARK: Lose yourself in the repetition: Overlap your circles, make them different sizes, fill them with color... don't worry about the outcome.

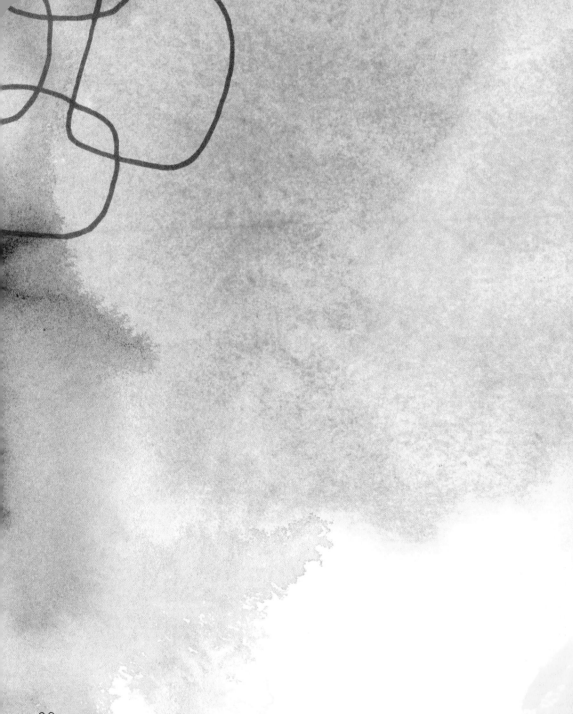

IDEA SPARK: See where the squares take you. Can you connect them to form something else?

Now try the previous exercise with squares. Instead of harsh, pointy-cornered squares, doodle squares with rounded corners like marshmallows.

HiP tO BE A
Rounded Square

23

24

Peace

Doodle/collage what peace means to you. Use symbols, words, or pictures.

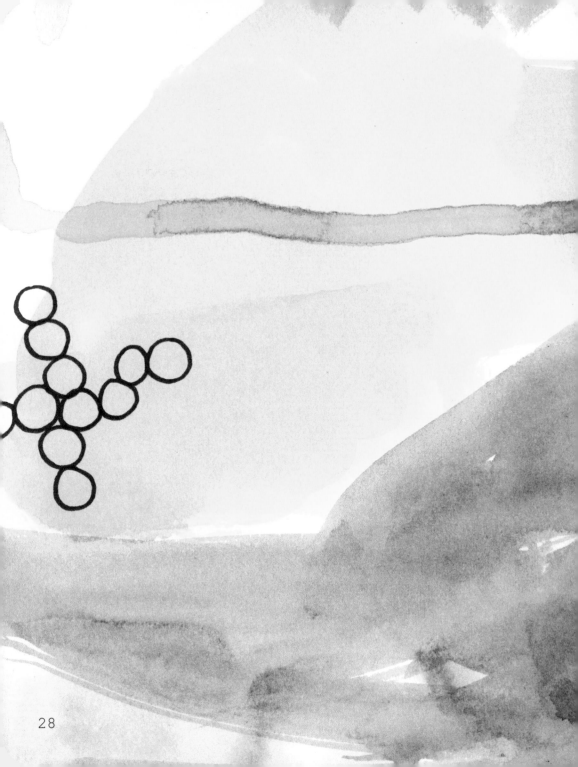

Create flourishes across these pages. Connect one to another until the page is full.

Curly
CUE

if YOU
DO WHAT YOU
love,
it is THE BEST
way
to RELAX.

— Christian
Louboutin

Doodle only in the colored areas.

35

Leaf it

Imagine a huge tree filled with branches and leaves. Doodle or collage those leaves, one at a time.

DOODLE Flow

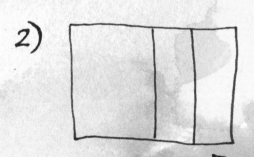

1)

OR

2)

1) Fold the opposite page in half toward you, either horizontally or vertically. If folding horizontally, tear the page halfway down, then fold.

2) Doodle all over the page, making sure to doodle continuously over the folded edge on the page behind it. Once you finish doodling, unfold your half and turn the page over. You should have part of the doodle you just created on half of both pages. Using your doodles as starters, continue the unfinished doodles until the entire two pages are filled. Try something different this time!

IDEA SPARK: Unfold the page after you turn it so you can doodle over the blank surface, too.

doodle

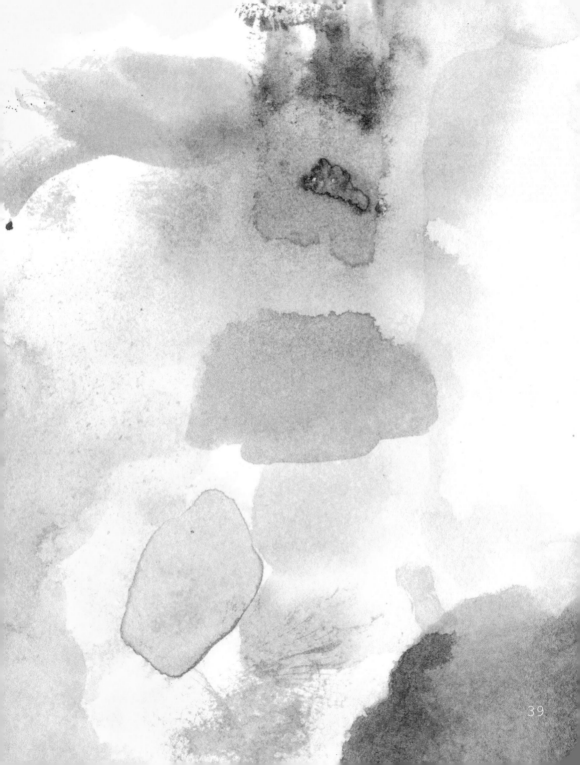

39

Doodle what you
See in these dots.

Sketch or scribble with
a relaxing color. Try
adding other colors,
one at a time, to make
a calming colorscape.

COLOR therapy

MANDALA *magic*

Mandalas represent wholeness. Doodle a mandala on the page to the right using the colors and the "starter doodle" in the center as a guide.

Wanderlust

Turn on relaxing music or some music that puts you "in a groove." Let your mind wander while doodling on these pages.

IDEA SPARK: Try doodling some themes from the songs, or doodle abstractly how the music makes you feel.

take a line

for a stroll.

Doodle all over the page without taking the tip of the pen off the paper.

Doodle Only in the white areas.

IDEA SPARK:
Match your pens
or markers to
the colors that
are already here
on the page.

Peace
IS NOT MERELY A
DISTANT GOAL THAT
we seek,
BUT a Means
BY WHICH WE
arrive
at that GOAL.

—Martin Luther King, Jr.

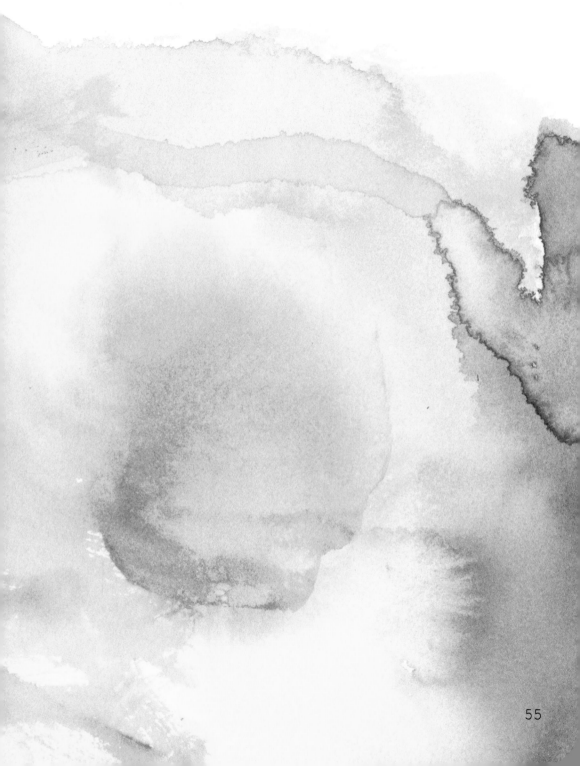

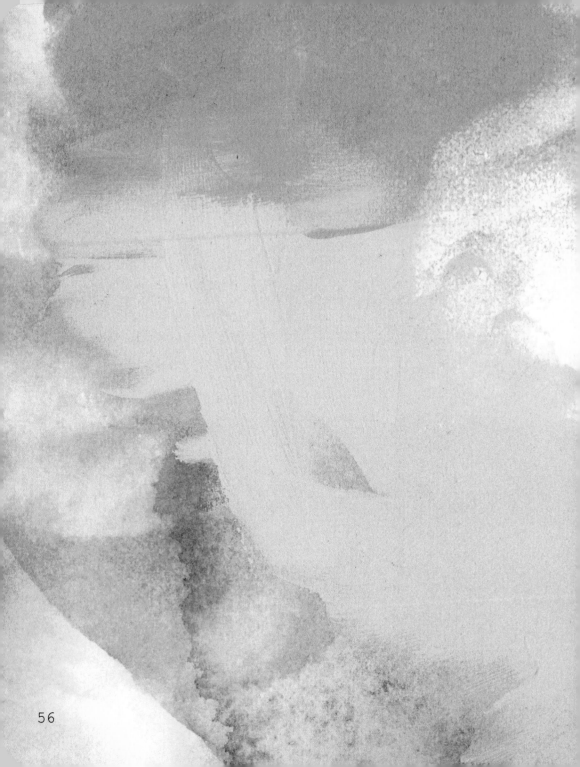

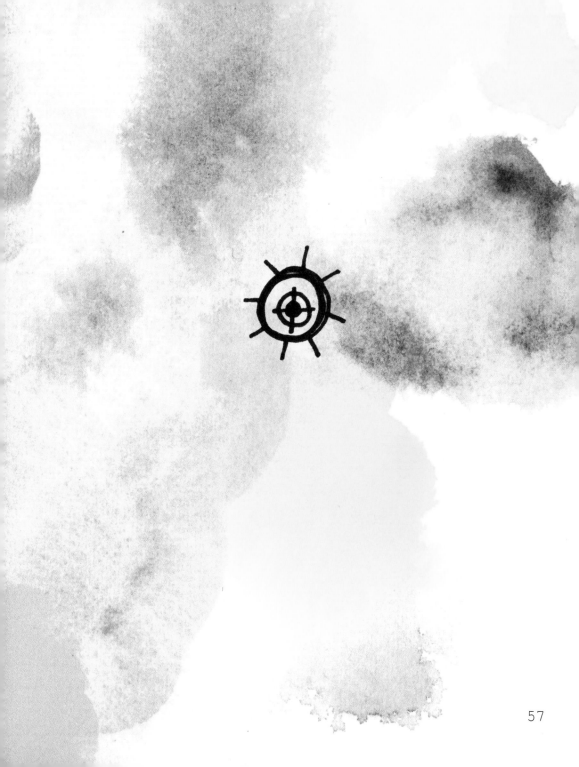

PURE
paisley

Let your pen pour paisleys all over the page.

IDEA SPARK: Use the dots to shade your shapes, or connect the dots haphazardly to create something new.

En Pointe

Doodle with just dots.

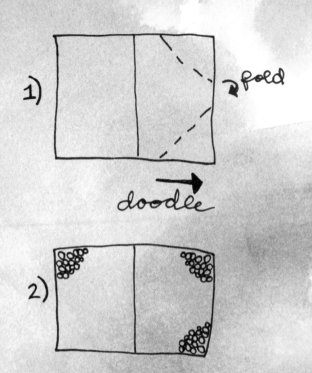

1) fold

doodle

2)

DOODLE Flow ^{2}

1) Fold the upper and/or lower corner of the opposite page toward you. Doodle all over the remaining surface of the page, making sure to doodle continuously over the folded edge onto the page behind it.

2) Once you finish doodling, unfold your corner(s) and turn the page over. You should have part of the doodle you just created in the upper and/or lower corners of both pages.

3) Using your doodles as starters, continue the unfinished doodles until the entire two pages are filled.

IDEA SPARK: Think abstractly
or find a nature scene. Whatever
brings you calm.

Serene
SPRING

What elements of nature do you
see within these pages? Doodle
from the textures and colors.

69

NO GREAT ARTIST EVER
Sees things
AS THEY REALLY ARE.
IF HE DID, HE WOULD
cease to be
an artist.
—Oscar Wilde

74

chapter 2

Slowing Down and Seeing

This section is all about taking the time to appreciate your surroundings. Whether you choose to observe reality or fantasy in this section, all of your marks are relevant. Don't try to draw realistically if you don't want to—doodling is what you want it to be. Make it imaginative. Make it you.

take a walk

What do you see around you? Doodle some of the shapes you see on these pages. Keep doodling around those shapes until the page is covered.

outside.

IDEA SPARK: Use a Uni-ball Signo or a white Soufflé pen over the dark areas.

LIKE a
Bird

You are a bird, floating
on air currents. What
do you see below?

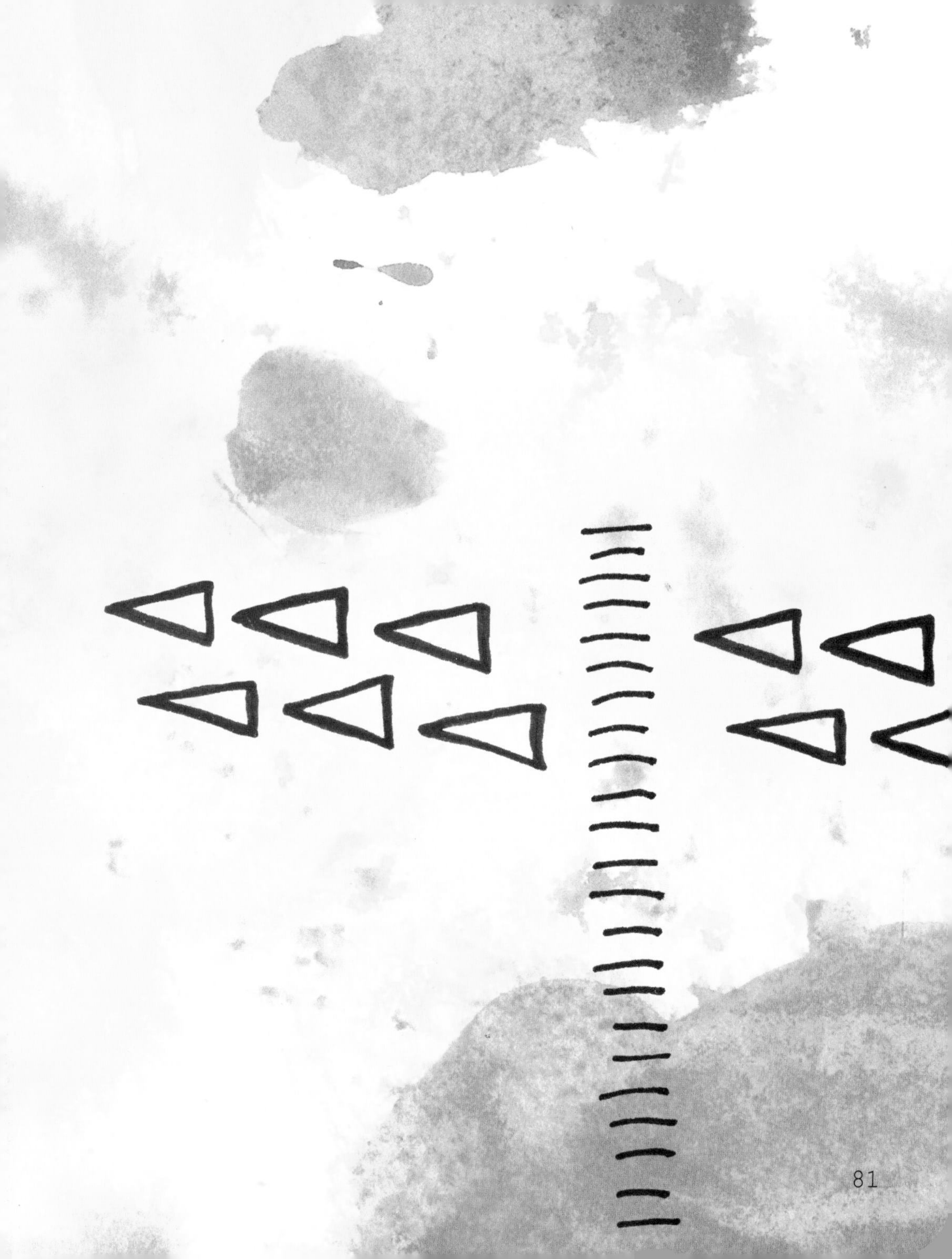

Little Things

MEAN A LOT

Doodle the tiny
details that can
make life wonderful.

84

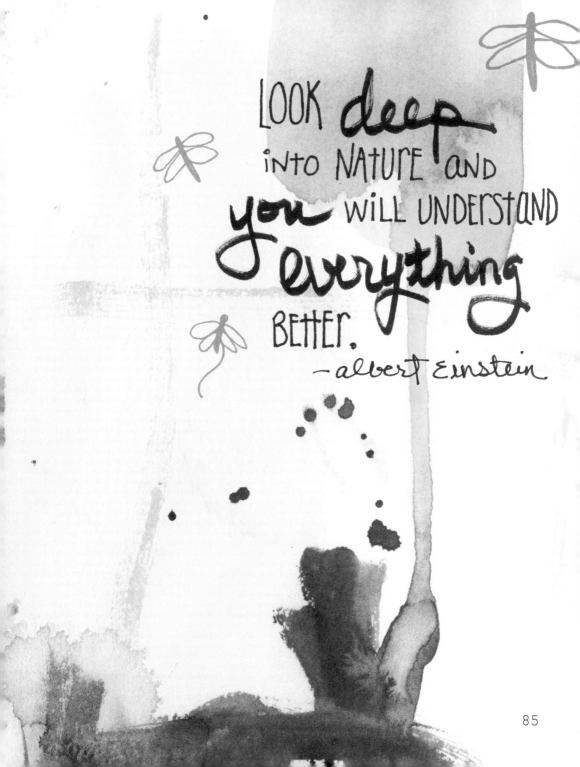

LOOK *deep* INTO NATURE AND *you* WILL UNDERSTAND *everything* BETTER.

— albert Einstein

HEAD IN THE clouds

On a cloudy day, lie back in the grass and gaze up at the clouds. What shapes and/or scenes are in those clouds? Doodle them here.

IDEA SPARK: It's best to look at clouds that are puffy and shapely!

Dive IN

Imagine you're scuba diving along the ocean floor. What do you see?

THE GREATEST SELF IS a
peaceful smile,
tHAT ALWAYS SEES
the *world*
SMILING BACK.
— Bryant H. McGill

IDEA SPARK: Every box can be like a happy little snapshot of your day. Make sure to doodle something that made you content.

Doodle something in each "box" every day for eight days.

Field
TRIP

Venture out to a park, a museum, or somewhere there is an abundance of activity. What do you see that makes you smile? Doodle, list, or collage it.

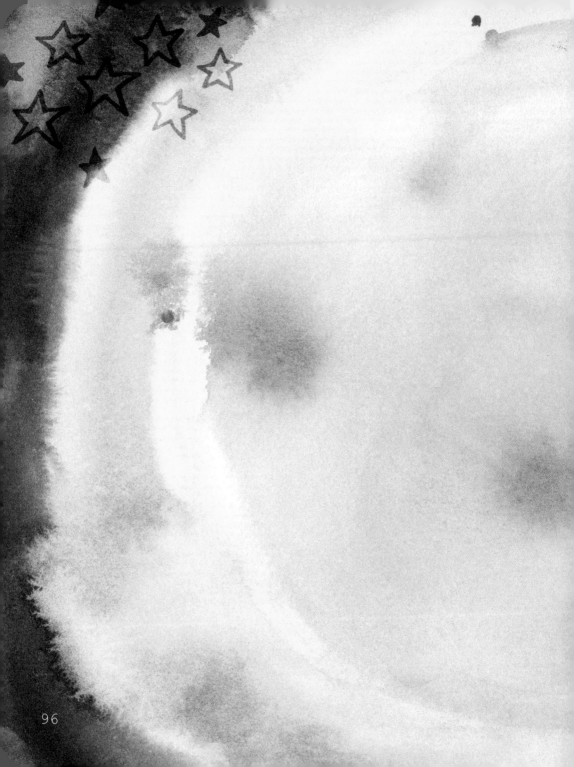

THE
doodles
IN OUR
Stars

On a clear night, do
a little stargazing.

Ocean
MOTION

Imagine yourself at the ocean, listening to the waves lap back and forth. Let the waves you draw reflect your current emotions.

IDEA SPARK: Are
your waves calm?
Turbulent?

EVERY BREATH WE TAKE,
every step
WE MAKE, CAN BE
filled WITH
PEACE, JOY AND
serenity.
~Thich Nhat Hanh

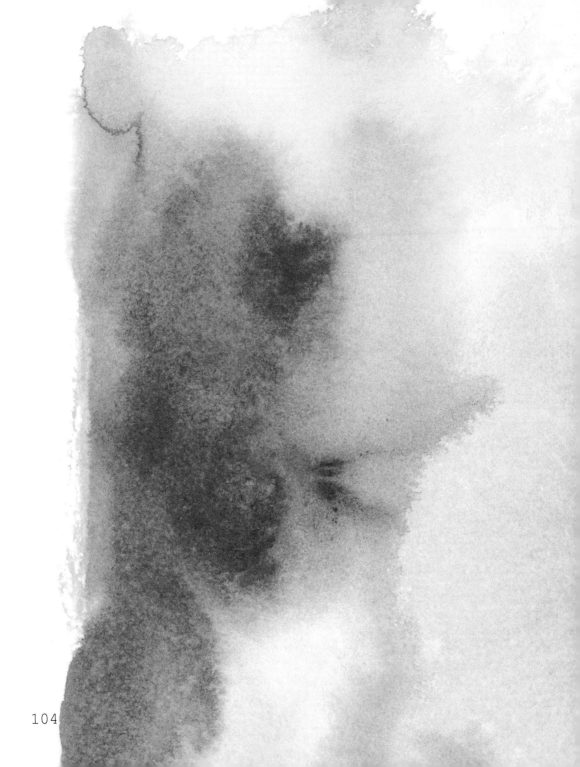

Collage and doodle ...

Tear out pages 107-108 and cut them or rip them apart into collage pieces. Glue them onto this and the resulting facing page in a pleasing composition. (Don't think too much about how you place them.) Then doodle over the whole thing to bring it all together.

ARTISTS WHO SEEK
perfection
IN EVERYTHING ARE those
WHO CANNOT attain
it in
anything.

~Gustave Flaubert

peace
COMES FROM
within.
DO NOT SEEK it WITHOUT.
~Buddha

chapter 3

Finding Your Zen

ZEN: n. noun An approach to an
activity, skill, or subject that
emphasizes simplicity and intuition
rather than conventional thinking
or a fixation on goals.

Now that you're loose and thinking about
the world around you, it's time to look within and discover your zen. These prompts will
allow you to be more introspective and take
stock of who you are and who you want to be.
Take a deep breath and jump in!

Doodle/list all the
wonderful things about
yourself. You deserve
some self-love!

Love THYSELF

Forgive
AND FORGET

Don't hold on to anger. Calm begins with forgiving those who've upset you. Doodle and write down the negative forces you're holding on to and what you need to do to let them go.

118

IDEA SPARK: Once you're done spilling, doodle positive influences and images over the negative.

AFTER A
storm
COMES A
calm.
- Matthew Henry

IDEA SPARK: When you feel as if you're "done," look at your page. What do you see there? Do you see people, buildings, or animals? Continue to work over the lines to transform them into shapes or things you recognize.

The best way to overcome uneasiness is to let go of what you know. Here, you will relinquish the control your sight has over your hand. Shut your eyes and move your pen around the page for approximately one minute.

Let Go

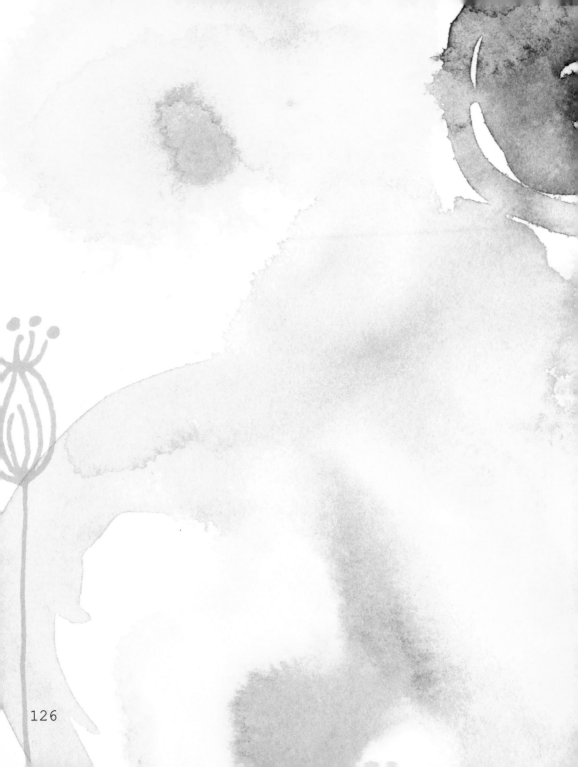

Follow THE NOSE

The sense of smell links powerfully to our memories. What smells bring on happy memories for you?

NOISY
Niceties

Sounds that make me smile:

IDEA SPARK: Which
sounds calm you?
Try to doodle those
sounds or doodle
the way they make
you feel.

Spiral SPILL

IDEA SPARK: To follow the spiral, turn your book as you doodle.

Using the spirals as guides—starting in the center and moving outward—doodle about your day. Allow one thought to flow to another. Fill in the colored areas with words, symbols, and icons.

My happiest, most relaxed moment in time:

happy, happy

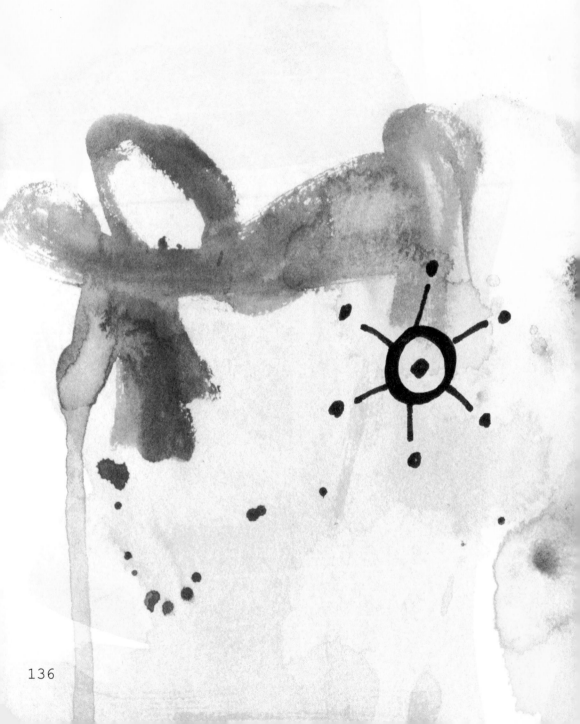

WHEN YOU FEEL A
peaceful joy,
THAT'S
WHEN YOU ARE
near truth.
~Rumi

dream state

What is the most
calming dream
you've ever had?

Serenity
NOW

What are some things you can do to
create more tranquility in your life?

Think of all the good things you see happening to you
down the road. Either doodle or write them as a list.

blissful FUTURE

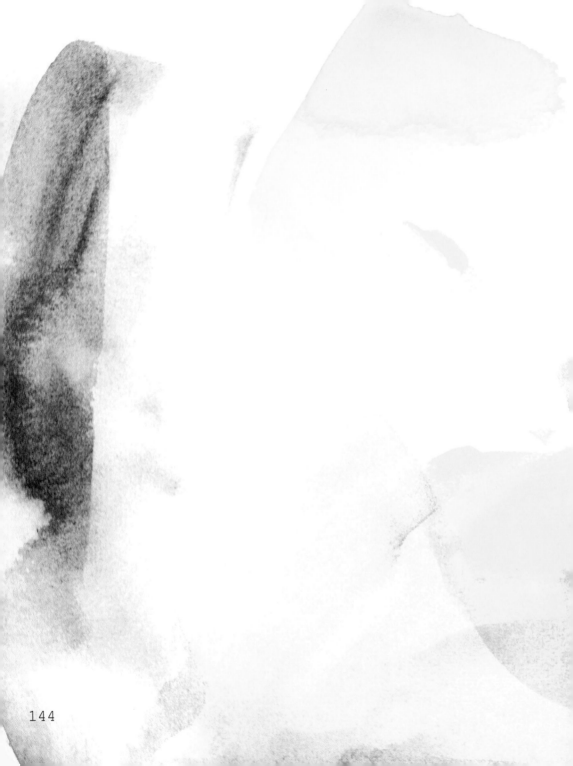

144

JUST BE *Still*

Find a quiet place in nature or a "quiet" corner. Doodle a symbol or icon that soothes you. Repeat it all over the page and let your mind go.

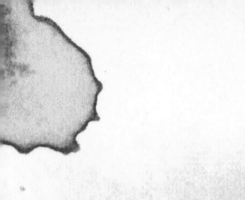

IdEA SPARK: Use your favorite pen or marker, one that feels good in your hand. Draw over your doodles slowly to refine them or add to them.

Art ENABLES US to *find ourselves* AND LOSE OURSELVES AT THE SAME *time.*

~Thomas Merton

IDEA SPARK: These words can be about you or the world around you. Focus on any words that make you feel good.

150

WORD
Wonder

Words can have a calming effect. What are some words that bring you peace? List or doodle them.

Collage
CALM

Find images of things that calm you and glue them on the page. Write what it is about them that you find so soothing. Doodle, too!

Funny FACE

Observe the people around you and doodle their faces and/or emotions. How are their expressions affecting you? Use the background shapes as beginnings of the faces.

Beauty SURROUNDS US.
~ Rumi

157

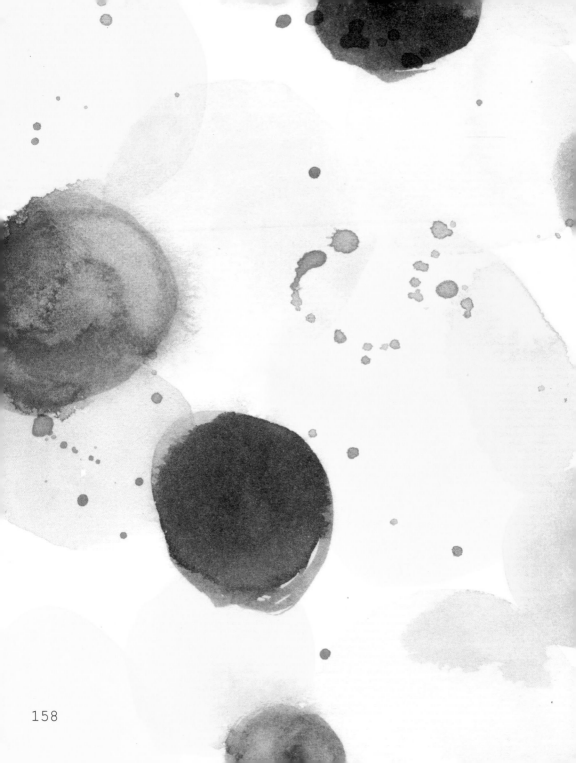